MATCHLESS G3L & G80

Keith Jackson & Deryk Wylde

CONTENTS

Foulis

Haynes

ISBN 0 85429 455 4

A FOULIS Motorcycling Book

First published 1984

© Haynes Publishing Group

Published by:
Haynes Publishing Group
Sparkford, Yeovil,
Somerset BA22 7JJ

Haynes Publications Inc.
861 Lawrence Drive, Newbury
Park, California 91320, USA

British Library Cataloguing in Publication Data

Jackson, Keith
    Matchless G3L and G80 super profile. —
(Super profile)
    1. Matchless motorcycle
I. Title II. Wylde, Derek III. Series
629.28'775 TL448.M3

ISBN 0-85429-455-4

Editor: Jeff Clew
Cover design: Rowland Smith
Page Layout: Teresa Woodside
Photographs: Peter Robinson and authors
Road tests: Motor Cycling and
EMAP National Press Ltd.
Printed in England by: J.H. Haynes &
Co. Ltd

Titles in the *Super Profile* series

Ariel Square Four (F388)
BSA A7 & A10 (F446)
BMW R69 & R69/S (F387)
Brough Superior SS100 (F364)
BSA Bantam (F333)
Honda CB750 sohc (F351)
MV Agusta America (F334)
Norton Commando (F335)
Sunbeam S7 & S8 (F363)
Triumph Bonneville (F453)
Triumph Thunderbird (F353)
Triumph Trident (F352)
KSS Velocette (F444)
Vincent Twins (F460)

Austin-Healey 'Frogeye' Sprite (F343)
Ferrari 250GTO (F308)
Fiat X1/9 (F341)
Ford Cortina 1600E (F310)
Ford GT40 (F332)
Jaguar E-Type (F370)
Jaguar D-Type & XKSS (F371)
Jaguar Mk 2 Saloons (F307)
Jaguar SS90 & SS100 (F372)
Lancia Stratos (F340)
Lotus Elan (F330)
MGB (F305)
*MG Midget & Austin-Healey Sprite
(except 'Frogeye') (F344)*
Morris Minor Series MM (F412)
Morris Minor & 1000 (ohv) (F331)
Porsche 911 Carrera (F311)
Rolls-Royce Corniche (F411)
Triumph Stag (F342)

B29 Superfortress (F339)
Boeing 707 (F356)

Harrier (F357)
Jaguar (F438)
Mig 21 (F439)
Mosquito (F422)
Phantom II (F376)
P51 Mustang (F432)
Sea King (F377)
Super Etendard (F378)
Tiger Moth (F421)
Vulcan (F436)

Great Western Kings (F426)
Intercity 125 (F428)
V2 'Green Arrow' Class (F427)

FOREWORD

Most motorcycles have some form of innate identity which is particular to the model or, in some cases, to the make. In the heyday of the big Matchless singles, the late 1950s, most enthusiasts would be able to recognise many of the popular machines of the day before they even had sight of the machine. The plodding beat of the big Panther, the somehow ineffective bark of the C10L and C11G 250 cc BSA machines, the regular beat of the 350 cc BSA B31, the booming note with a real sense of power from the Velocette Venom or Viper. In the midst were two groups of real enthusiasts with total loyalty to their own favourite brand of machinery but unable to tell the two makes apart except by relatively close visual inspection.

The two makes, AJS and Matchless, exhibited the first real examples of what was later to become known as badge engineering in the motor industry. Yet the enthusiastic owners, who knew that most of the parts were identical and that the machines were manufactured side by side in what was, at the time, the largest factory in the world devoted to motorcycle production, remained loyal each to their chosen brand.

The manufacturers were Associated Motor Cycles Limited, based in Plumstead Road, London SE 18, close by the Woolwich Arsenal and they were as much a party to the brand loyalty by dint of circumstance and history as by any considerations of improved market share or purely commercial considerations. Indeed, there remains no real record of why the separate identities were maintained to the end.

But separate they were and in this book we shall examine the history and the development of the Matchless-badged machines. In some cases the two marques did not share the badge, a prime example being the racing machines of the post-war period. The 350 cc overhead-cam single was sold only as the AJS model 7R whereas the 500 cc derivative was always raced as the Matchless model G50. The same was true in a limited sense of the off-road competition models. By and large the factory teams rode AJS versions in trials and the Matchless versions in scrambles, but it was not a hard and fast rule since works riders like Ted Usher and Artie Ratcliffe rode with a Matchless badge on their trials machine tanks and Geoff Ward's scrambler was usually an AJS. Maybe they, like the owners of the machines, felt that it wasn't just badge-engineering but that their marque was superior! Whatever the truth of the machine selection was, the origin of the actual models is easier to trace and most would agree that, in the case of the heavyweight singles from AMC, the original machines from which the later models were derived were the Matchless versions. The factory in Plumstead was building Matchless products long before the Stevens family were forced into liquidation and sold the AJS marque and models to the Colliers, owners of Matchless Motor Cycles Limited (later changing the name to Associated Motor Cycles Limited). Indeed, if you talk to any of the employees who worked in the factory until the shut-down in 1967, you will often find that they still refer to their employment as 'working in the Collier factory in Plumstead'. Equally, the engineering philosophy of the pre-war AJS machines in Wolverhampton and the Matchless models from Plumstead was significantly different. The AJS singles were often esoteric designs more suited to the cossetting care of the race mechanic, whereas the Matchless models of the thirties were essentially just sound, everyday machines.

It was that basic engineering quality with no frills and no nonsense which became the hallmark of the Matchless heavyweight singles. It is the same basic quality which has kept many of the machines in relatively regular use almost twenty years after production ceased and over forty years after the birth of the best-known Matchless single, the model 41G3/L War Department special which was the 'Forces Favourite' for many thousands of Despatch Riders in the second World War.

The writing of this book would not have been possible without the help and co-operation of many members of the AJS and Matchless Owners Club, who checked facts, loaned machines for photography and gave frank and forthright comment throughout the writing. Particular mention should be made of Graham Dean, whose knowledge of the wartime machines prompted research into previously unpublished details, Basil Chilvers, whose Matchless machines of the late thirties still carry him several times each year on trips of over 1000 miles to vintage vehicle rallies in Europe, and Ken Hallworth of the Vintage Motor Cycle Club to whom all motorcycles are a way of life.

Particular thanks are due to the helpful staff at the Public Records Office, Kew, and to the Librarian of the BP Library in the National Motor Museum at Beaulieu.

The majority of the photographs used were commissioned for the book and taken by Peter Robinson. Additional material was provided by the BP Library and by Mary Wylde.

**Keith Jackson
Deryk Wylde**

HISTORY

The motorcycle is a phenomenon of the twentieth century and the name of Matchless Motorcycles was held in high esteem for over sixty years as manufacturers of successful specialised competition models and ultra-reliable everyday machines. A product of the sporting aspirations of the two young sons of a general engineer with a small factory in the South Eastern suburbs of London, there remains no record of who dubbed the models with the name Matchless. But Matchless they most certainly were, in the literal sense of the word, since the earliest days of competition amongst motorcyclists. Indeed, the very first Tourist Trophy race organised in 1907 was won by young Charlie Collier riding his 432 cc overhead valve model. Matchless had arrived!

It is significant that the Matchless machines were designed, tuned and raced by the two young Colliers personally, who no doubt carried much of their determination to succeed back into the control of their father's factory. The first three years of the TT results show examples of that determination. Having won the 1907 event Charlie was favourite to win the 1908 but his luck was out on the day and he had to be content with second place behind Rem Fowler on the Norton. The

1909 event would therefore prove whether that first race win had been a lucky fluke or whether the machines really were Matchless. Both Charlie and Harry Collier entered and, after a race-long duel with the Nortons, emerged victors with Charlie taking first place a few yards ahead of brother Harry.

Racing results certainly helped to sell motorcycles, business boomed in the Colliers factory and the company grew. The early machines used other manufacturers engines since the family were competent general engineers but most certainly not engine design engineers. As the business grew so they began to attract other young engineers with ideas but their plans were dashed by the onset of the first World War. The factory was turned over to the manufacture of large V-twins for military use plus a series of engineering sub-contracts for the nearby Woolwich Arsenal.

After the War production for the public continued with the V-twin as the flagship of the range, fitted with either a MAG or a JAP engine. Plans for a new single were also well advanced, the model L – a 350 cc sidevalve single introduced for the 1924 season. The Press were taken aback, the first Matchless single since the War had been heralded as a Matchless-engined model, yet the L had a Blackburne engine. The Blackburne engine had been a last minute substitute when trials of the Matchless engine had proved unsuccessful. When the Matchless engine arrived in the following year their reviews were very critical, particularly since it took the form of an overhead camshaft single with the camshaft drive running up the rear of the cylinder and resulting in an unusual skewed cylinder head with a very exposed carburettor. However critical those first reviews, the first Matchless single had arrived and the heart of the engine, the crankshaft and flywheels that gave a stroke of 93 mm, was to apply to most of the

Matchless singles until 1963.

The engineering team produced a new model for the 1927 season, designated the T/S. The machine had an upright single cylinder engine with enclosed pushrods on the timing side and the rockers in a grease-filled box. The exhaust was the fashionable – if inefficient – two port system and the carburettor was mounted on a stub, tucked away at the rear of the cylinder. The Press liked it and gave it good reports for it was conventional. The public read the reports and bought the model. Although good racing results still sold a few specialist sports models, good Press reports sold the everyday models and that was where the profits were made.

The new model retained the basic bottom end with the 93 mm stroke. With the flywheels mounted on a single roller bearing on the drive side and a simple bronze bush for the timing side axle, the ancestor of the Matchless singles had arrived. More importantly, it had been accepted and gone into real quantity production.

During this period the Stevens brothers in Wolverhampton were also designing and manufacturing motorcycles but they concentrated on more sporting versions with many essays into the production of overhead camshaft models and heavy involvement in racing activities. An analysis of the real market had not been made and the sparse sales of very-well-thought-of sports models coupled to the high cost of running a full racing team brought about their financial downfall. Colliers, who had gone public in 1928, were able to purchase the AJS company and add selected items to their range.

In the early years of the thirties the two model ranges were obviously dissimilar but gradually all the ex-Wolverhampton exotica were dropped and the steady 93 mm stroke workhorse engine carried on, to appear also in certain AJS models.

The first 500 cc model with the 93 mm stroke bottom end was announced in 1933. It also heralded the introduction of a positive feed of oil to the rocker box through an integral tapping from the oil pump to a pipe supplying the rocker arms. Excess oil in the rocker box filled a well, which fed the inlet valve through an adjustable orifice. The remainder of the oil drained back to the crankcase down the push rod tubes. The engine also featured two ball bearings on the drive side.

The very first of the G3 models, which lasted in one form or another until motorcycle production ceased, was announced in April of 1935. It was a 350 cc with the classic 69 mm x 93 mm engine, having an upright cylinder and a Lucas magneto mounted at the rear. The bottom end had the twin ball bearings on the drive side to which reference has already been made. The overhead valves were closed by hairpin valve springs and the model had a sporting characteristic embodied in what amounted to a thoroughly practical everyday design which, in basic format, was to last for over thirty years, including arduous service in a World War when it was arguably the most popular despatch rider's machine ever known.

The introduction of the G3 model also heralded a change in Matchless policy that was to become a feature of the range – the adaptation of one basic design to suit the market needs of several types of rider, from ride-to-work through to outright competition. There was a G3 Clubman in road trim, with flared black-enamelled mudguards, a steel toolbox mounted to the rear of the gearbox and a low level exhaust as standard but with an upswept optional version. The G3 Clubman Special was intended mainly for competition use and was fitted with narrow, chrome-plated mudguards, and different wheels with competition tyres and modified front forks. The exhaust was

upswept as standard, which resulted in the need for tool-pouches fitted to the mudguard stays. The Clubman Special also had a rear and a prop stand whereas the Clubman had only a centre stand. All models were fitted with full lighting equipment and a Burman four-speed foot-change gearbox. The Special had a choice of internal gear ratios to suit the specific competition need.

A more significant introduction was the completion of the range in the Autumn of 1935 with the introduction of 250 cc and 500 cc variants. The 250 cc was an anomaly which was later dropped and does nor fall within the scope of this book but the 500 cc model was the first G80. Thus the Matchless heavyweight singles, the 93 mm stroke G3 and G80 models, were born. An interesting innovation in that first year of production was that the G80 Clubman and G80 Clubman Special models were each offered either in standard tune or, for £5 extra, with polished engine internals and a high compression piston. I'll wager that not many standard versions were sold but records do not exist to prove the point!

The 1937 models were provided with new cylinders and heads which were claimed to give better cooling. The rocker-box was given a direct oil-feed from the front end-cap of the oil pump chamber. The 350 was brought into line with the 500 by the inclusion of an oil-flow adjuster to the inlet rocker feed. Strangely, a twin-port version of the 350 was never made even though the 500, until 1939, existed in both twin-port and single port forms. The Super version of the Clubman Special, with polished internals, was given a different designation and thus was known as the model G90. The 1937 models are easily recognised by the large trapezoidal rocker covers. Less conspicuous changes included new wheels with a better brake and a new big-end assembly with a two-piece

crankpin and three-row roller bearings. The petrol tanks of the Clubman range, which had been black with gold lining on the 1935 models, were now chrome-plated with gold lined black panels and had gold lined tool boxes and mudguards.

The Matchless mould had definitely been cast since the range of models shared a common bottom end for the 350 cc and 500 cc engines and many cycle parts. Development work continued, but concentrated on one aspect at a time, rather than a complete model. This resulted in further changes to the Super cylinder head for 1938. The hairpin valve springs were modified to allow them to intersect around the valve stem and operate on the opposite side of the stem, thus reducing the overall clearance required around the springs. This permitted enclosure of the springs inside the cylinder head. At the same time the model designations were changed, the Super Clubman Special version of the G3 being introduced in single port version only as the G4. The G90 version was listed as a twin-port. For the first time all models were fitted with 14 mm spark plugs and a new petrol tank, holding three gallons, was fitted. The G4 and G90 models had a red tank panel, as well as red and gold wheel rim lining. The mudguards for all models gained a strengthening rib. The crankcase design common to all models – was improved by the inclusion of an oil feed beneath the oil-pump end cap rather than below the pump chamber. Of all those basic changes the one that most 'experts' emphasize is the change to the metal tank badge which received the well-known wings on the single 'M'.

During the years just before the second World War subtle changes took place in the organisation of motorcycle competitions, particularly with regard to off-road events. No longer was it solely a question of reliability; most manufacturers could offer machinery which would last through to the end of an event so the inclusion of special sections that demanded greater rider skill in path picking necessitated a change in approach to machine development. Matchless responded by redesigning the bottom end of the engine to contain much heavier flywheels, retaining the 93 mm stroke, to provide totally different power characteristics. This called for new crankcase castings. The Clubman models all received the Monoblock cylinder head even though both twin and single ported versions were still available. For the first time the competition versions were offered with detachable lights having a waterproof plug below the headlight. The finish on the machines was unchanged — but the Publicity Department had the last say. What had been described as 'red' in 1938 became 'Aldwych Red' in 1939!

The next few years in the Colliers factory were to prove traumatic. Before the outbreak of war in September 1939 Matchless had supplied machines for military use and many had assumed that when hostilities finally commenced Plumstead would be in the van of manufacturers of military motorcycles. Indeed there were already military versions of the G3, culminating in the 40/G3WO. But these were little more than ruggedised versions of the basic road machines bought in small quantities for forces that were fulfilling a peacetime role. The main contracts for large quantities of military machines were placed with Triumph, BSA, Norton, Ariel and Royal Enfield. The Matchless models were rejected.

To this day, no-one knows the real reason for the rejection. A popular comment was that the machines were too heavy, yet a close look at the successful Norton and BSA models makes that claim seem somewhat flimsy. It seems more likely that the proximity of the factory to the Woolwich Arsenal persuaded the War Department

Contracts Office that an order for Plumstead would be pointless, since they were already aware that the Germans intended massive bombing raids and that this corner of London was obviously a prime target. The factories in the Midlands may have been considered more safe from this risk.

For 1940 a model range was introduced that lacked all the competition models but included a selection of roadster models fitted with a new single down-tube frame which was claimed to improve both road-holding and steering. All the models retained the chrome-plated petrol tank with the Aldwych Red panels and gold lining.

The development engineers, led by Bert Collier, brother to Charlie and Harry, had been incensed by the weight comment. It was decided to develop a motorcycle which would be lighter, more manageable and more reliable than anything else available in Britain. They had been impressed by the performance of the pre-war BMW machines which had a telescopic front fork so a machine was purchased from the BMW distributor in Dublin and the forks were stripped and analysed. It was fortunate that one of the engineers had sound knowledge of the hydraulic technology and they were able to copy and then improve upon the design. A sign of the times was the use of light alloy for the fork sliders — nobody was going to call Matchless machines too heavy again! Sadly, the copying of the BMW forks resulted in personal tragedy, after the machine had been reassembled and was being evaluated in a longer term test by Bert Collier. On the way in to the factory one morning, he and Jack Kelleher had a private race and the BMW did not make the turn at the foot of Pol Hill. Bert was killed instantly and the British motorcycle industry lost one of its most promising innovators.

The engineers had also noted the comments of the Wheeled Vehicle Experimental

Establishment who had evaluated the potential of a 1935 G3 Clubman as a military motorcycle in a 10,000 mile test. Inspection of the internals at the 8000 mile mark revealed that the hardened cap on the inlet valve had been lost and that both pushrods were bent. There was significant wear on the hairpin spring collars and the springs themselves had distorted. The factory noted the problems and developed the 40G3/WO, which was effectively the Matchless G3 with the cylinder barrel and enclosed coil spring head of the AJS model 16 at the time. One vital criticism remained, the machine was too heavy, so a 250 cc version was supplied for evaluation in 1940. It was lighter but scored badly in terms of predicted reliability and maintenance under military use since the high compression engine had been tuned and fitted with light flywheels to give a power peak at 6,000 rpm, making the power output comparable to that of the 350 cc machines supplied by other manufacturers. The motorcycle had to be completely redesigned, so the factory set to with a privately funded development and fitted their new Teledraulic front fork to a new frame with a much-lightened version of the coil-spring engine from the G3/WO. The G3/L was born, some 60 lbs lighter than its predecessor. Although the War Office had bought small quantities of the G3/WO and then ordered small quantities of the G3/L, the major orders from the Ministry of Supply still went to the Midlands manufacturers. The night of 13th November 1940 changed all that when German bombs destroyed the Triumph works in Priory Street. Everything was lost, machines, spares, machine tools and most of the actual tooling. Triumph's loss was Plumstead's gain and orders for the new model, now designated 41G3/L flowed in. It was lighter, faster and infinitely more comfortable than its girder-forked compatriots. One historian described it later as 'probably the highest degree of development of a single cylinder motorcycle for military use.'

There were slight model variations on some of the Ministry of Supply orders, but, on the whole, the model remained fairly consistent throughout the War.

When peace was restored, the factory resumed production in July 1945 of two models, both of which were intended to meet export demand before being released on the home market. The 350 version was the 41G3/L with a black finish and some chrome plating to relieve the monotony. It had a bigger carburettor and road-going ratios in the Burman CP gearbox. The 500 was virtually the pre-war AJS model 18 engine with the magneto fitted to the rear of the cylinder, in similar cycle parts to those of the 350. The use of the model 18 engine precluded the standardisation of crankcase and other engine parts. Evidence of development was provided by a new timing side shaft, oil-pump plunger and guide pin assembly, designed to double the oil flow-rate and reduce wear on the plunger and pin. The oil passages were also enlarged to allow the greater oil flow and a shorter con-rod was fitted, the gudgeon pin bosses in the piston being lowered by an equivalent amount. This was intended to reduce the heavy bore wear which had first been criticised by the War Office in 1935! Externally, there was virtually no change in appearance apart from a little extra chrome and new lining styles. In 1948 a competition model was introduced to meet the demand for trials use. The competition model started with an all-iron engine but was shortly offered with alloy cylinder head and bronze cylinder head conversions, then an alloy cylinder barrel to further reduce weight and dissipate heat under the rigours of competition. To this day there is confusion over the alloy barrels since many enthusiasts claim that

the factory made their own barrels and Wellworthy produced their Alfin component for owners to fit to iron-engined models. In fact Wellworthy made all the barrels but the ones they supplied to the factory were designed to be fitted to the 'bolt through' type of crankcase, in which long studs from the crankcase passed through the cylinder barrel to meet up with sleeve nuts in the cylinder head. The version sold for fitting to existing machines used an identical barrel, but had the cylinder base specially machined so that it would accommodate the arrangement used on the standard iron engine.

As the competition model emerged with its all-welded frame, a new range of road models was announced with a slightly longer wheelbase to cope with the increased average speeds as road surfaces improved and the benefits of better fuel were realised. The need for improved braking performance necessitated dropping the small $5\frac{1}{2}$ inch diameter brake drums in favour of the 7 inch units which had been used just before the War. The small brakes had been necessary as part of the weight reduction exercise for the 41G3/L.

A mid-season change gave the 350 and 500 cc engines a common bottom end, which was also used on the equivalent AJS models. Now the only difference between AJS and Matchless, other than badges and colouring, was the inner and outer timing chain covers, which dictated placing the AJS magneto in front of the cylinder and that of the Matchless at the rear.

For 1949, a spring frame was offered on some home models and the designation S added to the model type. The earliest springers were fitted with AMC's own design of rear suspension unit with a relatively small oil reservoir. They soon became known as candlesticks, and revealed a tendency to lose their damping function due to the fluid frothing which made them rattle abominably on rough surfaces.

They also leaked badly. In their favour it should be noted that the clevis-end fixing used for many years by AMC is a far superior fixing to the normal overhung versions. Also in 1949 the coil springs for the valves were discarded and the hairpin springs reintroduced. Other detail changes were made but the next one of any significance was the adoption of alloy heads for both the 350 and 500 cc engines in 1951, and the introduction of an optional spring frame for the competition models, which were supplied with alloy barrels as standard for the first time. The new spring frame sported the Mark II Teledraulic rear suspension units. Still clevis-ended, a new internal design eliminated the overheating and frothing problem by having a much larger oil reservoir. The enthusiasts immediately dubbed them 'Jampots' because of their shape. To this day the AJS and Matchless Owners Club magazine is called 'Jampot' a reflection of the universal acceptance of the AMC engineering standards in their determination to do things their own way.

Many students of design look upon 1952 as the season when badge engineering at Plumstead became a reality. Not only was the magneto position rationalised on the AJS and the Matchless models but many more of the cycle parts were shared not only by the two heavyweight singles, but also by the twin cylinder models.

Works support for competition in the early fifties still showed an open-handed allegiance. There were both AJS and Matchless factory teams in trials and scrambles. Later, in the sixties, the allegiance swung towards Matchless only scrambles teams, mainly because such a move halved the expense. The effect of the Teledraulic fork design and the lightening to suit the military market and give a much more manageable competition motorcycle is perhaps best seen by looking at the results of the most prestigious trial in the British calendar, the Scottish Six Days.

Between 1932 and 1939, AMC are featured only twice, when George Rowley came equal third in 1932 and when Fred Povey came third in 1937.

After the War it was a totally different story. In 1947 Hugh Viney won it on an AJS and Artie Ratcliffe came second on the Matchless. The following year, 1948, saw another win for Viney on the AJS and again in 1949. 1950 saw a radical change. Artie Ratcliffe won on a Matchless and Hugh Viney came second on an AJS!

In 1951 Artie took third place on a Matchless and in 1952 a newcomer to the team, Kentish farmer Gordon Jackson took third place on an AJS. By 1953 the winning ways had returned and Viney won the trial on an AJS with a loss of 35 marks, just three points ahead of young Gordon Jackson, also on AJS. 1954 was Artie Ratcliffe's turn to win on a Matchless.

From 1955 until 1964 there wasn't a single year without at least one Plumstead product in the first three, and often two. Included in the list is the famous win by Jackson in 1961 when he rode his AJS for six continuous days around the Highlands on the most demanding trials sections in the British Isles and put his foot down just once, in the whole week, to steady himself. That win with the loss of just one point on Grey Mare's Ridge is unlikely to be matched.

The 74mm x 81mm model was so obviously successful, that a major competitions dealer, Comerfords of Thames Ditton, telephoned Plumstead on the Monday morning after the Scottish and offered to place an order for a 100 Jackson Replicas. It wasn't just pure speculation because Gordon Jackson had stayed in the Highlands with his new wife for a fortnight's holiday and the machine had been brought back south in the Comerfords van. It was ridden on the Sunday in a South Eastern Centre trial and thoroughly evaluated by the enthusastic Comerfords staff. But the factory turned down the offer.

The public were astonished when the 1962 trials model was announced, still with the longstroke engine, still with the vulnerable $15\frac{1}{2}$ inch Girlings, still with the old heavy frame. They showed their disapproval with their wallets and Plumstead lost their credibility as suppliers of off-road competition machines virtually at a stroke. The scrambles machines had used a short stroke motor 86mm x 85.5mm since 1956, again not really within the compass of this profile, but it is interesting to note that the factory scramblers were very critical of the weight and poor handling of the standard frames compared to the superior characteristics of the frames supplied, for example by the Rickman brothers for their Metisse specials. When the factory finally responded and produced a new frame it was too late.

The standard road models also adopted the 74mm x 81mm engine for the 1962 and early 1963 seasons and were relatively successful, but the motorcycle market was changing. Various manufacturers, not the least those in Japan, had produced lightweight models of 250cc or thereabouts, which were faster and more economical than the traditional British 350cc single. Thus the factory sold less and less of the heavyweight singles. In 1964 an attempt was made to create an attractive package with the adoption of the 85.5 mm stroke engine in both 350 cc and 500 cc formats embodying many items common to the Norton range, which also had come into the AMC Group.

None of these ploys were successful, the longstroke Matchless 350 engine introduced in April 1927 disappeared in the summer of 1961, unknown to a generation of faithful followers. It has to be said that it wasn't really the competition from abroad that killed the British motorcycle industry but the totally unimaginative and unrealistic approach of the so-called professional managers brought in to revitalise it.

The building that was once the largest factory in the world devoted solely to motorcycle production has now been flattened to make way for a car park.

EVOLUTION

1933. A new 500 cc engine with an 82.5mm bore and 93mm stroke was introduced. It was fitted to a model designated the D/80 which became the forerunner of the Matchless heavyweight singles. It had an inclined engine, a twin-port exhaust system and positive lubrication of the rocker box from an integral tapping of the oil pump.

1935. A new 350 cc model, the G3 was introduced, based on the D/80 rather than the D/3. It had an upright single port engine with hairpin valve springs. The name 'Clubman' was used for the road model and 'Clubman Special' for the competition version, the latter having narrower chrome-plated mudguards, different tyres and forks. Optional gear ratios were available.

1936. The 'Super Clubman' versions were introduced, having 14 mm spark plugs and polished engine internals. The 500 cc designation G80 was used for the first time.

1937. The 'Super' designated models took on a new model number, to become the G90. All were fitted with new cylinders and heads. The rocker oil feed was taken from the front end-cap of the oil pump. The 350 cc version gained an adjuster in the inlet valve

stem oil feed similar to the one fitted to the 500cc D/80 model. The 1937 on engines are easily recognised by the large trapezoidal rocker cover. The year also saw the introduction of a two-piece crankpin. The 'Clubman' models had chrome-plated tanks with black panels, chrome-plated wheel rims with no paint stripe and a black toolbox, oil tank and mudguards with gold lining.

1938. A 'Super G3', known as the G4, was introduced. Having a new cylinder head design shared with the G90 model, it enabled full enclosure of the valve gear. All models gained new crankcases with the oil feed entry beneath the oil pump rear cap. All models were fitted with 14 mm spark plugs. A new 3-gallon petrol tank was fitted and the tank motif gained wings. The G4 and G90 models were finished with a red tank panel and red stripes on the wheel rims all bounded by gold stripes

1939. All models gained the monoblock head fitted to the 1938 G4 and G90 models. Larger flywheels were fitted to the 500 cc models, which required new crankcases. The competition model gained a QD headlamp. The finishes were the same as in 1938.

1940. Despite the outbreak of war a civilian range was announced for 1940 with a new single down-tube frame. The competition models were dropped. The military models were not announced, but in 1940 the first contracts for the 40/G3WO were placed.

1941. All civilian production ceased. Some contracts for the 40G3/WO remained valid but the main production was of the 418G3/L which retained that designation for the duration of hostilities. The 41G3/L used a lightened AJS model 16 engine with coil springs and a rear-mounted magneto.

1945. The announcement of two models in July revealed a civilian

version of the 41G3/L with a black finish relieved by some chrome plated parts such as handlebars, levers and filler caps. It had a bigger choke carburettor. The 500 cc version used a 1939 AJS model 18 engine in the same frame, fitted with a rear-mounted magneto. As the models did not share a common crankcase, different engine plates were required. The finish was in black enamel with a transfer in place of the pre-war winged-M motif. The lining was unusual in that it ran around the sides of the tank in the style later adopted on the competition machines. According to the literature of the period there is a black pinstripe, but photographs first published in June 1946 show examples of the familiar 'D' shaped panels, some with a pinstripe and some without. It is impossible to determine which finish is technically correct. The machines were fitted with grease-filled, Burman CP-type gearboxes, having standard road internal gear ratios rather than the wide ratio gears fitted to the WD models. Though introduced in July, these models were sold through 1946. In common with all British manufacturers the new season models were introduced in September of the previous year, in time for the London Motor Cycle Show. Thus reference to 1948 models means models manufactured between September 1947 and August 1948. The engine number series maintains this format and an engine produced in October 1947 will be numbered as a 48/G3L.

1947. The main design change was the adoption of a new timing side main shaft and oil pump plunger, with enlarged oil feed pipes and passages, to give twice the previous oil flow rate. A new, shorter con-rod was fitted and a new piston with lowered gudgeon pin bosses. The roller bearing on the timing side was replaced by a flanged bronze bush. A competition model was supplied to the works riders but did not become available to the public until mid-season. It has a cast iron engine, with the option of an alloy or bronze cylinder head. A 21 inch front wheel and alloy mud guards were fitted and the exhaust system was upswept at the rear.

All the models had the same black finish but made increasing use of chrome plate. The wheel rims were chrome plated with black centre lines and a silver pinstripe. Competition rims were never painted.

1948. The roadsters appeared with a new longer wheelbase frame. Not visible was the change in the method of damping the Teledraulic front fork with a freely-floating shuttle in the base of the fork leg rather than the fixed piston connected to the fork top-bolts since 1941. Externally, the forks had new top-shrouds with combined fork brackets for the headlamp rather than the four separate strips fitted previously. The petrol tank had a handsome chrome finish with Aldwych Red panels similar to the pre-war units but with a silver line in preference to the gold. The oil pump plunger was enlarged again, as was the guide pin, requiring a slightly different crankcase. A welcome change was the return to the 7 inch diameter brake drums which required a different alloy fork slider with two bosses to take the brake plate locating bolts. A mid-season change introduced after engine number 8000 was the use of the the complete 500cc bottom end on both the 500 cc and 350 cc models. At the same time an engine numbering anomaly was introduced with the adoption for a short period of the designation G80L rather than just G80.

1949. The greatest change for the season was the announcement of an optional spring frame version to be known as the G3LS and the G80S – note that the G80L anomaly was withdrawn on the springer but remained on the rigid framed model. The spring frame

design was AMC's and the rear suspension legs utilised a similar damping mechanism as the front forks.

New cylinders and heads were fitted, with valves controlled by hairpin valve springs. The valve-lifter was transferred from the exhaust tappet, where it was prone to oil leakage problems, to the rocker box, where it operated directly on to the exhaust valve operating arm. The oil-feed tapping was moved from its position just above the spark plug to a new position on top of the rocker box.

1950. The rigid framed models were modified to accept the rear hub fitted to the spring frame models. Surprisingly, the sprung singles were not fitted with the popular AMC twinseat, as were the G9 twins, but retained single saddles and pillion pads.

All models were fitted with steel crankpin bearing washers. The competition versions were completely revamped with the fitting of an alloy cylinder barrel and head as standard. They also had a five-spring clutch fitted, leaving the G3L as the only model in the range with a four-spring clutch. The 500 cc models had additional clutch plates to accommodate the extra power. The finish of the competition models was black, with a 2-gallon steel tank with silver lining around the sides and a metal motif.

1951. For the first time a competition version of the spring frame was available. It consisted of the competition front frame, of the all-welded construction common to all AMC competition models, with the standard road frame rear fitted. It proved universally unpopular because of the great weight increase over the standard rigid model. Even the works teams rode the rigid version. New to both road and competition models was the AMC Mk II rear suspension, using Teledraulic rear units – the Jampots. All models were fitted with the alloy cylinder head and

alloy pushrods to maintain valve clearances over the optimum heat range. On the competition models heavy duty Burman BA/type gearboxes were fitted. Wide gear ratios were used for the rigid models but most spring-frame models had the standard road ratios specified.

1952. Many changes to all models were announced. A new gearbox, the Burman unit known as the B52, was fitted. Developed from the racing units, it featured shorter, stouter shafts, larger bearings, fewer engagement dogs on the gears, and better wear characteristics. The clutch withdrawal was by means of ball bearings mounted between dimpled plates which gave a very smooth and progressive action. The smaller cases of the new gearbox eased the access to the dynamo so the magneto was moved to the front of the cylinder to make complete dynamo access possible.

On the road engines a new cylinder design was incorporated with a thicker base flange and no compression plate. The hairpin valve spring design was changed from a short-legged spring, which required a special tool to remove and fit the springs, to a longer-legged version operating on a simple steel tray, which meant that strong-fingered mechanics could strip and assemble the valves wtihout the use of tools.

The electrics became positive earth for the first time and the cables were colour-coded.

One of the biggest changes which causes most problems to restorers who prefer to maintain original standards was the limitation on chrome plating enforced by the then-current shortage of tin. AMC used a silver-coloured stove enamel finish on wheel rims, fork covers and rear suspension covers which they termed 'Argenised'. Unfortunately AMC used several suppliers of the silvery stoving enamel, which has resulted in several standards being available for present day matching. It is a source of much discussion amongst enthusiasts.

A different style of Lucas headlamp was selected, with a square block pattern lens and a suspended 'gondola-style' parking light under the main body. The upper fork yoke was modified to have three fixing screws in the handlebar clamp and a slightly longer upper spring cover was fitted.

1953. For the first time the AMC twinseat was fitted to the spring-frame models, the rigid frame models retaining the single saddles. The UK models still carried the Argenised finish but export models were supplied with chromed units. An invisible modification was the change of the upper and lower front fork shrouds, which were modified so that the fiddly fixing screws and plates were discarded and the shrouds held in place by the clamping action of the fork springs. A useful innovation was the adoption of extended fork stops which were drilled to enable the fitting of a locking bar and padlock when the machine was parked.

1954. The road models reflected the easing of the post-war austerity with a general revision to increase performance. Higher compression pistons were available as an option and all models were fitted with a different cylinder head with larger ports to improve breathing and a suitably increased carburettor choke. On all but the trials models the flywheel weight was reduced and the HL (high lift) cams previously fitted only to the scrambles models were fitted all round. The G80 and G80S models were fitted with a Lucas SR1 rotating-magnet magneto, with an automatic advance/retard mechanism fitted under a bulge on the timing cover. With plating again possible, the tanks were enamelled as standard, with a chromed version as an option. The wheel rims were chromed with a black centre and silver pinstripes on the

UK models and a red centre with silver pinstripes on the export models.

A new alloy front hub was fitted, a full-width unit using straight spokes. The whole range gained new frames, with a different swinging arm being used on the springers. For the first time the rigid tourer had a different front end to the springer and the competition models had their own rear frame which gave an extra 2 inches ground clearance. The headlamp design changed again to a unit with torpedo-shaped parking lights on either side of the headlight unit. This was the first year of the moulded-plastic tank badge.

1955. All road and trials models were fitted with an Amal Monobloc carburettor. The 350 cc road models also gained the Lucas SR1 magneto similar to the 500 cc unit but with a different advance/retard mechanism.

New frames were fitted to the road models with a different style of rear sub-frame which incorporated extensions for the pillion footrests and included a mounting for a sidecar fitting. New front forks were fitted to all models with $1\frac{1}{4}$ inch stanchions instead of $1\frac{1}{8}$ inch. The alloy fork sliders were restyled in a much smoother design. Front and rear alloy hubs were a new full-width design and the rear was made quickly detachable. The headlamp design was unique to AMC and comprised two separate pieces with a rearward extension to carry the speedometer. The lighting switch and ammeter were symmetrically arranged in the headlamp top. The front mudguard was a new design with internal bracing to eliminate the front stay. The machines had a sleeker appearance. The rear suspension units were also improved – they can be recognised by the circlip below the bottom spring cover in place of a nut.

1956. For the first time there were no rigid models listed or available as options. This enabled the frame

design to be stiffened and the alloy casting which connected the engine plates, front frame and rear sub-frame to be discarded in favour of a lug on the seat tube which was now placed vertically. The oil tank and toolbox on the roadsters were redesigned to fill the loops on the rear sub-frame and the twinseat was extended rearward to cover the upper rail and forward to blend more with the tank. With new large transfers on the toolbox and oil tank, the appearance looked even sleeker.

The scrambles models adopted the short-stroke motor and thus drop out of this profile at this point, although it is interesting to note that the very last Matchless single offered for sale was the G80CS in 1967!

1957. A major change occurred in the adoption of an in-house gearbox instead of the Burman design used for so many years. Design students will trace the conversion of a Norton gearbox to the AMC unit – and will remember that the Norton was really a Sturmey-Archer.

The clutch contained a shock-absorber so the engine drive shaft could be shortened and stiffened. Girling rear suspension units were fitted but the AMC clevis fixing was retained. Restorers are therefore faced with finding ways of modifying standard Girling units themselves since the clevis-ended ones went out of production years ago. For some unaccountable reason the G80S shared a new frame and twinseat with the twins, whereas the G3LS frame is the 1956 unit, modified to take the Girlings, and has a different seat and oil tank. On both models the oil tank and toolbox covers have six small ribs and a flat central area carries the small Matchless laurel leaf transfer offset by fine gold lines on the rib crests. The laurel leaf transfer is a work of art, with seven different colours in the design. It is the subject of some rather poor four colour copies and only the Owners

Club has genuine reproductions at the time of printing. The primary chaincase for 1957 is unique for the year, with a small front dome and considerable efforts made to improve the sealing against oil leaks.

1958. The major change was the adoption of a Lucas alternator and coil on the roadsters in place of the separate dynamo and magneto. The alternator was fitted in a new alloy primary chaincase and the timing cover, which differentiated between AJS and Matchless models, disappeared to be replaced with a simple housing for the contact breaker points. The headlamp lost its torpedo parking lights and gained a parking bulb mounted in the pre-focus unit, just below the main bulb.

The finish of the models included an option of off-white tank panels or a black frame and forks, silver mudguards and petrol tank, and red tank panels, oil tank and toolbox.

1959. A new frame for the trials models provided more ground clearance and was $1\frac{1}{2}$ inches shorter. Weight reduction was achieved by the reintroduction of the $5\frac{1}{2}$ inch brakes and front fork of the old 41G3/L model. The rear suspension used the same $15\frac{1}{2}$ inch Girling units as the recently introduced G2 and G5 lightweight models. The forks had alloy top yokes. The road models were mechanically unchanged but their designation was changed to G3 and G80 and four colour options were listed for the UK market. Deeper mudguards were fitted.

1960. A new duplex frame was fitted and a larger ($4\frac{1}{4}$ gallon) petrol tank. A new, longer dual level seat was used, identified by its white bead. The G80 cylinder head was redesigned to give better gas flow to improve mid-range power and the internal gear ratios were revised to give a smaller gap between bottom and second. The second to third and third to top gaps were equalised. The finish was the same as in 1959.

1961. The major change was the reversal of the colour finish options. Items that had been red were offered in white, and vice-versa. The plastic tank motif was enlarged and a broad outer band incorporated. Internally, the oil pump drive was improved.

1962. The long-standing 93 mm 350 cc engines were dropped in favour of a short stroke unit and therefore drop out of this profile, as far as road going versions are concerned. The trials models retained the longstroke engine and went unchanged for the 1962 season. The G80 models continued unchanged but sold in pitifully small numbers.

1963. The trials models received a slight review with the change from a Dunlop rubber competition saddle to a simple foam pad unit. The new model names, Maestro for the trials model and Major for the G80, announced in 1962, continued to be ignored by virtually all owners and the press. The road model was given 18 inch wheels with new full width alloy hubs which incorporated wider ($1\frac{1}{8}$ inch) brake shoes to give much imroved braking. For the first time they did not use taper-roller bearing, a long standing AMC hallmark.

A larger ($4\frac{1}{2}$ gallon) petrol tank was fitted with a silver zig-zag lining and the large cast motif first used in 1962. The oil tank and toolbox were of new shape and the rear frame was modified to take standard Girling suspension units instead of those with clevis ends. To suit the new wheel radius, new mudguards were fitted with a squarer cross-sectional profile and a central rib. A new silencer of different shape and with improved noise reduction characteristics was introduced. There was an optional enclosed rear chaincase for the model. The only finish available was black and silver.

It was to be the last year of the genuine Matchless-engined models with the 93 mm stroke. In 1964 all used the 85.5 mm short stroke engine fitted to the scramblers since 1956. It was, in effect, a hybrid version of the shortstroke scrambles unit with a Norton oil pump fitted. The models were unpopular, AMC were in severe financial difficulties and they lost the goodwill of the dealers who had supported them with advice which had been almost totally ignored. The range continued for another $2\frac{1}{2}$ years, but it was no longer the Matchless that had once been famous.

SPECIFICATION

A brief explanation of the factory numbering system will help prospective purchasers determine just what is being offered. In the case of the longstroke singles the task is relatively simple insofar as determining the year of manufacture. The Engine number stamped on the drive side crankcase just below the cylinder barrel includes the model year. It should be noted that AMC made the changes to their models in the Autumn to coincide, generally, with the London Motor Cycle Show. Hence models manufactured after September will bear the following year number in their designation.

Dealing with the post-war models, a 51/G3L/1234 would be a 350 cc rigid road model built between Sept 1950 and August 1951. Similarly a 55/G80S/12345 would be a spring frame 500 cc model manufactured between Sept 1954 and August 1955. The clue to the spring frame version lies in the S in the Engine Number; a rigid frame 500 would have had a designation such as 53/G80/3456.

One of the commonest mistakes lies in the description of the competition models. Firstly *all* competition models have the designation C both in their engine and their frame numbers. By and large the spring frame competition versions were not used for trials until 1955, and most of the competition models supplied by the factory were in scrambles tune with a high compression piston and road ratio gearbox internals. Thus a model designated G3LCS or G80CS is almost without exception a scrambles version. The trials models were designated G3LC and G80C up to the introduction of the lightweight frame in September 1958, when they became the G3C. It is not believed that any 500 cc trials models were made in that frame since the longstroke 500 competition motor had been dropped in August 1955.

The numbering system of the frame is more complicated since the frames were numbered during manufacture and then passed to the general assembly area at which time they received the engine and marque designations. It is therefore possible to give only the earliest number used during any year but no indication of the model from the number. The numbering series is:

Year	Number
1946 (from Sept 1945 to Aug 1946)	500
1947	12760
1948	23358
1949	35000
1950	47000
1951	59744
1952	74100
1953	89501
1954	–
1955	A21057
1956	A37700
1957	A49350
1958	A59492
1959	A66800
1960	A72300
1951	A76550
1962	A83900

Transmission

The heavyweight singles used the same chain sizes throughout the period, the primary being $\frac{1}{2}$ in x 0.305 in and the secondary $\frac{5}{8}$ in x $\frac{3}{8}$ in. Gearing changes were made primarily by changing the engine sprocket, although wide ratio gears were also available and used as standard in the competition machines. The rear wheel sprocket had a standard 42 teeth on *all* models and the gearbox drive sprocket always had 16 teeth. On Burman clutches the sprocket had 40 teeth and on the AMC clutch it had 42 teeth.

The standard engine sprockets are as follows:

15 teeth – optional low gear sprocket for 350 cc sidecar models
16 teeth – standard trials sprocket for 350 cc trials models 1948 to 1955
17 teeth – 1947 350 cc competition models and post-1956 350 cc trials models
18 teeth – standard on 350 cc road models with Burman clutch, including WD41G3/L and also on competition 500 cc models with Burman clutch. Sidecar 500 cc.
19 teeth – standard on road 350 cc models with AMC clutch
21 teeth – standard on road 500 cc models with Burman clutch.
22 teeth – standard on road 500 cc models with AMC clutch

Internal Gear Ratios

Model (gearbox type in brackets)	1st	2nd	3rd	4th
41G3/L (CP)	3.09	2.28	1.29	1.00
Road 1945-1951 (CP)	2.67	1.76	1.28	1.00
Trials 1945-1951 (CP, BA)	3.16	2.09	1.29	1.00
Road 1952-1956 (B52)	2.65	1.70	1.31	1.00
Trials 1952-1955 (B52)	3.11	2.02	1.42	1.00
Scrambles 1952-1955 (B52)	1.87	1.35	1.09	1.00 (Close ratio option)
Road 1957-1959 (AMC)	2.67	1.77	1.35	1.00
Road 1960-on (AMC)	2.56	1.70	1.22	1.00
Trials 1957-on (AMC)	3.24	2.44	1.56	1.00

Special note: Many owners using trials machines in current pre-65 events are not able to find wide ratio gears. However the proportional difference between first and second as well as between second and third is almost the same on both road and wide ratio gears, the only real difference is the large gap between third and top on the trials set to give reasonable performance on the roads. Since pre-65 trials rarely use the roads, it is quite feasible to use road gears suitably lowered by means of sprockets. It is common to fit a 15 tooth gearbox drive sprocket and 13 or 14 tooth engine sprocket. Some owners with the Burman clutch have a 46 tooth sprocket made for the clutch in place of the standard 40 tooth unit.

Suspension

Owners of the pre-Girling spring frame models can obtain complete rear suspension rebuilding kits from the Owners Club Spares Scheme or from most of the specialist spares suppliers. Similarly, the Owners Club Spares Scheme has manufactured all of the replacement parts for the Teledraulic forks except the alloy bottom fork sliders. Even these units are currently under consideration.

Colour Finishes

Accurate restoration of the Matchless red colours is difficult since the factory purchased paint from more than one source and there are definite differences that can be detected even across models of a single year. The Owners Club maintains lists of acceptable paint shades currently available.

Lubrication

The Matchless lubrication system was designed and then proven empirically before the days of readily available multigrade oils. There is considerable discussion amongst Matchless owners as to whether it is preferable to use the traditional mono grade oils available currently from several specialist oil manufacturers as well as from most filling stations in the Elf chain. The consensus of opinion favours this course of action if only because there are obvious differences of opinion exhibited amongst the industry experts.

ROAD TESTS

Publishers Note
It is not possible to include road tests of the post-war G3L and G80 models because the manufacturer placed an embargo on all road tests after a magazine had published a somewhat critical report that offended the Joint Managing Director. Fortunately, *Motor Cycling* conducted a road test on a new military model, which was supplied for this purpose by the Army in 1941. This report is therefore published in lieu.

This photograph of the new G/3L clearly shows the new Teledraulic fork, the slimmer engine and exhaust system, the neat arrangement of pillion seat and rear carrier and the single but commodious toolbox.

A NEW MILITARY MODEL TESTED
The 350 c.c. Model
Modified Gear Ratios, a Remarkably Flexible and the New Teledraulic Fork Combine to

THE introduction of a new model is a big event in these troublesome days, but our readers must not imagine that, because such announcements are so few and far between our manufacturers are letting any grass grow under their feet. Their main object at the moment is to assist, to the utmost limits of their capacity, the country's prosecution of the war. That, in the main, means the building of thousands upon thousands of motorcycles. These have to be turned out with precision and promptness and any sudden and radical changes in design would seriously interfere with the steady flow of production. Modifi cations and improvements must be incorporated from time to time however, and, as our readers are aware, the objects of such changes of recent months have been the reduction of weight, combined with easier handling and snappier performance. It was, therefore, with considerable interest that we "took over" for test the latest and slimmest line in the Matchless range—a model destined for the Army, having successfully passed the rigorous tests through which the military authorities put all such machines.

The New Fork

It is known as the G/3L, for it is substantially a lightweight edition of the well-known G/3—the 350 c.c. overhead valver which has been doing such excellent work in the Army. Besides being much lighter, however, it boasts a number of major improvements, the most outstanding being the new Teledraulic front fork, the innermost details of which are still on the secret list.

The general layout of this new fork is obvious from the photographs accompanying this report. It operates on the telescopic principle and incorporates coil springs

allied with a hydraulic system which absorbs road shocks and also dampens the "rebound." The springs only take the static weight of the machine; it is the hydraulic system that controls the "springing" when the model is in action. It gives a surprising range of movement (4½ ins.

(Right) A close-up view of the near side of the G/3L. Note the neat way the horn, magneto, dynamo and battery are mounted, and the clever prop-stand folded back behind the footrest.

(Below) The bottom end of the Teledraulic fork. The wheel spindle is effectively "nipped" by a bolt-up type split bearing. This sketch also shows the hand adjustment for the brake.

from "top" to "bottom"), but in actual fact the operational variations over normal surfaces are amazingly small. But before going into more details about the fork, let us introduce the machine as a whole.

That it looks lighter to the eye than does the G/3 is another state ment the veracity of which is borne out by the accompanying illustrations. Actually, approximately 60 lb. have been "lost," and this reduction in weight, combined with the Teledraulic fork, has produced a delightful, yet altogether different, machine. Carving 60 lb. off a solo without impairing its efficiency, affecting its reliability or robbing it of any of its power is no easy task, but by careful planning and development, Associated Motor Cycles, Ltd., have managed the job most successfully. For instance, by reducing the

May 15, 1941.

MOTOR CYCLING

This photograph of a G/3 Matchless from which the G/3L was developed, enables you to make an interesting comparison. That the latter is considerably lighter is obvious, whilst the Teledraulic fork looks very much more efficient and businesslike. The improved exhaust system should also be noted.

G/3L o.h.v. Matchless

Power-unit, Greatly Reduced Overall Weight Produce an Outstanding Services Machine

finning on the cylinder head and barrel some 4 lb. 10 oz. were saved. By dispensing with knee-grips another 1 lb. 14 oz. were "removed"; the absence of a steering damper deleted 1 lb. 3½ oz.; an alteration to one of the frame lugs saved 10 oz. and by employing only one toolbox a further 2½ lb. were added to the total. (This one toolbox, incidentally, carries not only as many tools as are now accommodated in the two boxes on the G/3, but the tools are of superior quality.) The massive appearance of the Tele-

draulic fork, too, belies its light weight, and both mudguards show a saving.

Other noticeable alterations include a smaller, and neater, exhaust system which is so tucked away that it is unlikely to suffer any damage in the event of a spill. It fits snugly against the crankcase below the timing chest and curves behind the footrest and below the gearbox casing, but above the bottom frame member. The footrests are minus rubbers—an unnecessary luxury in war-time—but the carrier has been moved farther to the rear to make room for a comfortable pillion seat. The special folding pillion footrests are also extremely neat, yet very strong and businesslike. The head lamp shown on the model tested is not of the type which will be fitted, although the method of mounting is correct. The approved lamp is much smaller and will be fed by a 10-watt D.C. dynamo without battery. (An alternating current unit was fitted at first, but was not considered

The pillion footrests are exceptionally strong and the rear-wheel speedometer drive equally neat.

(Left) [How the handlebars are mounted on the latest Teledraulic fork. Oil is fed into the tubes through the top nuts and the speedometer is mounted in front of the head.

good enough.) With full tanks this new machine weighs 319 lb. against the G/3's 375 lb.

"Cyclops" collected the machine from the works and put it through its paces. This is what he says about it:—

Excellent Handling

I have rarely been so impressed with a new machine as I was on becoming acquainted with the G/3L. The way it handled over the battle-scarred streets of London on the journey from the works to *Motor Cycling's* office—and that trip happens to embrace some of the most densely trafficked, and certainly some of the most evilly tram-lined streets, in the Metropolis—was a revelation. The model seemed to float along; that's the only word to describe it. Pot-holes; tramlines; in all their various stages of decay; irregular stone setts and hurriedly filled-in bomb craters, were smoothed out like magic by the Teledraulic fork. There was never a jar or a judder; just a sweet, smooth action

The lower of the two bridge pieces of the Teledraulic fork incorporates a sturdy head-lamp mounting, and, at the back, the fork stop.

50   MOTOR CYCLING   *May 15, 1941.*

which no combination of springs could ever achieve. There was no pitching or tossing, except very occasionally when the unsprung rear wheel objected to some particularly bad bit of surface which the front end had literally "smoothed out."

Another aspect of the journey which could not be ignored was the tremendous amount of interest the model created among other road users at traffic blocks. At the noted Elephant and Castle crossing a policeman descended upon me, causing me swiftly to think over my so far rapid journey. But it was not I who had attracted him; he had spotted the Teledraulic fork. "That's a new departure for the War Office, isn't it?" he queried. (Evidently the khaki colour of the machine was sufficient for him to associate it with the Army!)

"Yes," I replied, "and a jolly good one, too!"

"It certainly looks it. It does look right, doesn't it?" he carried on.

There, unfortunately, the chat had to end because I had received the signal to carry on and I was in a hurry. I couldn't help adding, however, as I slid off the mark, that 60 lb. had been carved off the weight of the machine. The glimpse I caught of him over my shoulder was one of an agreeably astonished bobby whose face also managed to convey a mixture of delight and envy. (I'd like him to have a ride on the model as a reward for his keen observation and enthusiasm.)

Super Suspension

For the next few days the model was used as much as possible, and it continued to delight. The fascination of that fork never receded into the background, although I found myself wishing, time and again, that the rear wheel had a similar suspension system. The model simply shrieked for Teledraulics fore *and* aft.

One very simple experiment was sufficiently conclusive proof of the desirability of rear suspension. I handed the model over to Editor Graham Walker and asked him to ride it over a 4-in. step. He did so, several times as a matter of fact, and it was most interesting to see how the front wheel appeared to "glue itself" to the ground, whereas the rear wheel, despite Graham's 15 stone, persisted in hopping 2 or 3 ins. into the air. And that was at speeds well below 10 m.p.h. (Perhaps the War Office will one day realize that neither the Germans nor the Italians scorn rear-wheel springing.)

Some action pictures of Graham Walker and "Cyclops" putting the G/3L through its paces over War Office testing ground. (Top, left) "Cyclops" breasting Red Road in second gear with plenty of power to spare. (Centre) Graham Walker negotiating a rough-surfaced cutting. (Left) The Editor deliberately picking the wrong path without any disastrous effects.

The G/3L's happiest cruising was in the vicinity of 50-55 m.p.h., a speed which it maintained in an effortless manner. Its maximum was, of course, considerably in excess of these figures; indeed, it would maintain 60 m.p.h. and over for long stretches without tiring in the slightest degree. The only noticeable difference was a sharper and louder exhaust note.

Starting was simplicity itself. When the engine was cold it was necessary to flood the carburetter slightly. (A slight criticism in this connection concerns the float-chamber tickler, which, besides being rather inaccessible, is much too close to the fuel tank's rear bridge-piece.) This done, the engine always started at the first kick. When warm, no flooding was required; in fact, it was fatal to do so. The air lever could be left fully open and the ignition did not need retarding to obtain "first-kick" results.

In due course I took the model over some of the War Office's own testing ground in the Bagshot Heath-Pirbright area, being joined on this occasion by Graham Walker, who was as keen as I to see how it performed on cross-country stuff.

Arriving early, I decided to do a little investigating on my own account and proceeded to experiment on the famous Red Road. The G/3L simply romped up in second gear. It tackled several other gra-

(Top, right) "Cyclops" tops a sharp rise. There was no crashing on the part of the fork when the front wheel landed, nor did it show any tendency to deviate from a straight line. (Right) A spot of quick motoring over some tree stumps. Notice the perfect alignment of the front and rear wheels, though both are off the ground, thanks to a succession of "steps."

dients in the vicinity in a similar manner, but what was even more pleasing was the extraordinary punch of the motor at low revs. When turning in a tight circle, or when the front wheel hesitated on a bit of roughery, the model could be "kicked" into position by merely a snap opening of the throttle. The response was instantaneous and certain, even on steep gradients. This slow-speed pulling is a characteristic that has received quite a lot of attention and the results are good and very desirable in a machine which is used for such a variety of jobs with the Services.

Another obvious improvement over the G/3 was the altered gear ratios—5.83, 7.5, 11.75 and 18.4 to 1 as compared to 5 83, 7.5, 10.3 and 15.6 to 1 on the G/3. The lower first and second ratios make a tremendous amount of difference and, with the extra punch of the engine at low revs. there is no longer any need to rush hills, or, failing that, to slip the clutch, in order to get up—always providing, of course, that a reasonable amount of wheelgrip is available.

When Graham arrived we moved off to Pirbright, where the model was thoroughly tried out over all types of going. We put in hours at it and I was gratified to learn that my Editor shared my enthusiasm for the delightful way the G/3L behaved. Its lighter weight, snappier engine and more suitable gearbox have resulted in a most delightful machine which will captivate the most discerning rider.

There is, however, just one suggestion I should like to make, even though it means adding on an extra 1 lb. 3¼ oz. That is—replace the steering damper. Let me explain what I mean . . .

For ordinary work such a fitting is certainly not wanted. The machine steers perfectly and a damper, for road work, would be superfluous. The same remark applies to most forms of cross-country motoring, but there were occasions during our test when the model would have performed to better advantage if a steering damper had been fitted. One particular hill emphasized this point. It was a steep climb, loosely surfaced, with a sharp right-hand bend in it. The front wheel persisted in "wandering," and no amount of strength could hold it to the desired course to enable the bend to be tackled. A damper would have been of considerable assistance. As such obstacles are quite likely to occur in the life of a military motorcyclist, the provision of a damper is, I think, desirable, if only for such emergencies.

A Pleasing Model

This suggestion—it is not a criticism—is no reflection on the Teledraulic fork, which behaved on rough stuff just as superbly as it did on main roads. There is just a slight tendency to slide in deep sand, but this, again, would be cured with a steering damper. It smooths out the roughery in a surprising manner and the large movement available enables gullies, tree stumps and the like to be crossed without any crashing or "bottoming."

Cross-country riding, entailing a lot of first and second gear work and some fastish motoring at a consistent 60 m.p.h. to and from Bagshot, resulted in a petrol consumption of 54 m.p.g. Normal, everyday riding gave a consumption of 63 m.p.g., cruising being limited to the 50-55 m.p.h. mark. Oil consumption was negligible.

The brakes were well up to their work. Both were smooth in operation and decidedly positive. The front brake, thanks to the fork, was exceptionally good. The control lever is of the Bowden T.T. type (as is the clutch lever).

To sum up, the latest Matchless G/3L is a splendid machine possessing some very pleasing characteristics which will earn it considerable popularity. The Teledraulic fork is a winner, absolutely. May the day soon arrive when the rear wheel will also "float" along.

MATCHLESS
Clubman

Predominates wherever Motorcycles are ridden

Manufacturers of
**HIGH QUALITY MOTORCYCLES
FOR OVER HALF A CENTURY**

MATCHLESS MOTOR CYCLES · PLUMSTEAD ROAD · LONDON S.E.18

OWNER'S VIEW

Three members of the AJS and Matchless Owners Club, each with a penchant for Matchless models of a significant period, were interviewed using the same core questions as a guide. Each presents a different view but all shared the impression that the machines will last for many years to come.

Basil Chilvers lives in Cambridgeshire and admits that his favourite machines are the girder forked rigid models of the thirties. He has a small collection of models which includes an early model L sidevalve and a hybrid vintage racer which is now in regular competition use.

Graham Dean is keenly interested in the War Department models. Having been a Despatch Rider at an early age – admittedly after the hostilities – his thoughts are primarily practical. His researches into the military models are respected for the care and attention to double-checking the apparent facts.

Keith Jackson, whilst admitting that he would like to find a pre-war model to restore and ride, owns models which include the rigid telefork model so typical of the fifties and also later swinging arm models. A stalwart of the Owners Club he has held many posts but none more vital than his period of responsibility for the organisation of the Spares Scheme during which he – with the valiant help of his wife, Ruth, – analysed every AJS and Matchless part number for all the post-war models and organised a filing system which enables any part and all of its usages to be identified from the part number. A vital service when many of the models used the same parts.

The questions and answers have been summarised from several sessions.

Q. Why are you so interested in the Matchless singles?

B.C. I must admit that my interest, initially, was just in finding a vintage motorcycle! A friend in the office said that his Dad had a 1930s Ariel for sale and when I went to see for myself it turned out to be a 1937 AJS 250 cc – or, to be truthful, most of one. Advertising to find the necessary bits resulted in finding many spares, some of which were AJS and some were Matchless. I have been able to build up several machines from the bits and I am still finding old derelicts.

G.D. From the age of sixteen I was riding one for a living and I liked it so much that I bought an ex-WD model for my own use in the evenings and weekends. I was so impressed with it that I have retained a particular interest in that model.

K.J. More by accident than by design! As a youngster I found a Matchless single which I bought as a means of transport. A year later I joined the Owners Club and, with a friend, formed an East Midlands section. I think that my enthusiasm for the marque comes as much from being a member of the active club than anything else.

Q. When and why did you buy your singles?

B.C. In the early 1970s. In those days many of the old British bikes were available for very little money and I was able to establish a large stock of pieces.

G.D. Mine was advertised in a job lot of motorcycles for sale in Essex, just one WD model in the midst of a collection. I decided to buy it and restore it as an exercise in nostalgia. Having started, I seem to have become addicted to picking up old military models all over the place.

K.J. As soon as I had passed my driving test and saved up some money, I started hunting for a bigger bike. That was in November 1968. In the local paper there were a couple of bikes advertised within my price range, a BSA A7 and a Matchless G80. I went to see the Matchless first because three friends already had one! It was a 1958 G80S; I bought it and still use it regularly to this day.

Q. What condition were they in?

G.D. Most looked very rough on the outside but were in surprisingly good condition when stripped. It proves the basic quality of the original workmanship.

K.J. My G80S was in tidy external condition but the internals had suffered at the hands of previous owners. My 41G3/L, for example, was bought from a scrapyard in a dreadful condition for a fiver. That was in the early 1970s and spares in those days were very cheap so it was possible to rebuild it and remain solvent.

Q. What repairs/renovations have been done?

B.C. I have had to repair, modify or renovate almost every part of one or other of my machines. Being essentially a practical motorcyclist rather than a purist, I know that my adaptation of parts from one year model to another offends the purists but that doesn't detract from the pleasure that I get chuffing across France en route to meeting old friends at the rallying point.

K.J. In my case, apart from fitting good spares, the majority of the actual work has been in repainting and fighting off the demon rust. Apart from my initial troubles with the G80, which resulted in a rebore, new timing shaft and big-end, it is obvious that the Matchless engines and AMC/Burman gearboxes were typically over-designed so they are likely to outlast me! The wearing parts in the forks and suspensions seem to be one area that many owners overlook and yet they are relatively easy to maintain.

Q. Have you had difficulty in obtaining parts?

B.C. I call Joseph Lucas the Prince of Darkness partly because his products are not very efficient but mainly because, when they fail, they are almost the worst bits to replace. Also, I often wonder why replacement sleeves for the two-piece crankpins are not made instead of the modern one-piece replacements, which don't seem very reliable compared with the Matchless original quality.

G.D. Even forty years on there are still new spares in the maker's wrappings for many of the WD models; so far they are still relatively cheap.

Q. Has your machine won prizes in competitions?

B.C. Several times I have been awarded trophies at Continental rallies for being the farthest travelled entrant, even beating the trailered machines in many cases. But my pleasure is in the overall riding, not just the rallies themselves. I am also racing a vintage racer which started out as a 1939 model G3 and which has ended up with a 7R conrod and big-end in some specially fabricated steel flywheels. They fitted most easily into a pair of ex-WD crankcases and experiments to improve the performance and reliability have resulted in the use of a 250cc head. It is a real mongrel but the pleasure of being the first into the corner in a vintage race surpasses many other experiences at my age!

G.S. I don't really approve of concours competitions since many of the machines seem to be over-restored. To my way of thinking a restoration should be to full operational condition and that means relatively regular use which soon knocks the false super-shine off the concours models.

K.J. No. I don't restore machines to that standard. Both my wife, Ruth, and I ride the machines on a regular basis because we prefer to see them used rather than see them kept as some sort of museum piece. There are examples of concours machines that actually live in their owners' living rooms. We don't ride very often in the winter, however, when the salt on the roads eats through the irreplacable parts of a machine such as the original mudguards.

Q. Is there an owners club?

B.C. I regularly visit my local section of the Owners Club where there is at least one formal meeting each month and often other social gatherings as well. I also ride to meet other sections from time to time, I enjoy meeting with fellow enthusiasts. To me it is another example of maintaining standards that we all took for granted in the past. As an example, I had a crankpin break on my Matchless as I rode into the Ferry Terminal in France. I was able to get to the boat and hence back to England. A telephone call to ask a neighbour, who is also a club member, for advice, resulted in his bringing my car and trailer over 300 miles to collect me and the bike. To me that is real friendship.

G.D. My feelings can be summed up by the comment that, were it not for my membership of the club, I would probably never meet other WD Matchless owners.

K.J. I have been a member of the Owners Club for a long time and I have derived a great deal of pleasure from it. I have seen the Club grow from eighty to sixteen hundred members and marvelled at the constant increase both in interest and in the facilities which the club can offer. My own activities in helping to organise the Spares Scheme highlighted the poor quality of some of the early pattern spares that were offered and the vast reservoir of knowledge that is growing in the club should help to keep the quality of spares and information high long after the commercial interest in the marque fades.

Q. Is there a specialist that you find particularly helpful?

B.C. For me the sheer helpfulness plus the quality of speedy service that I get from Hamrax Motors, and 'Chopper' in particular, means that I rarely need to look any further. I suppose it is the way that they will offer advice on where else to try when they can't help that I find most impressive.

G.D. Over the years I have found that Russells have the best stocks of WD parts, indeed almost everything is still available by return of post. With that sort of service I am rarely tempted to look elsewhere.

K.J. I have had dealings with many of the suppliers of spares both as an ordinary member of the Club buying bits for my own machines and also in negotiation for the manufacture of obsolete items for the Club Spares Scheme. I have to agree with Basil and Graham that both Hamrax and Russells certainly do give excellent service and can supply most of the average user's needs.

Q. What advice can you give to potential owners and how would you sum up the enjoyment you get from your Matchless?

B.C. The best advice for someone contemplating buying a Matchless is don't buy one in bits unless you really know just what you should be getting. Many parts look as though they should fit but there are minute differences between models and years that could wreck a motor! I always feel that a whole model offered for sale should at least run and I am very suspicious of comments that minor work or adjustment will bring it happily to life.

My enjoyment lies in being out in the open on a motorcycle and being a part of the country through which I am passing. I also enjoy the friendship with kindred souls that generates from the use of my machines.

G.D. Advice to potential owners is simple. Find your machine, restore

it back to operational condition, preferably in full military trim if it is a WD model, and then ride it and ride it. My enjoyment comes from the pleasure of being out and about, unfettered by the constraints of being in a car. The models are easy to ride and, on modern roads, reasonably comfortable. You have to watch the braking though. It is nowhere near to modern standards. Don't worry about the reliability, I've never yet failed to get home.
K.J. My advice to a potential buyer would be to get advice directly from an owner if at all possible. There are many popular misconceptions that abound and it is better to talk to someone who may already have spotted some of the pitfalls. Don't be discouraged by this, on the whole most models that you can buy are totally straight, particularly if the original registration details of frame and engine number still correspond. Obviously some models will have had engine or frame changes for a whole host of possible reasons, many quite logical. The problem is that of

buying spares like, for example, seats or exhaust pipes. Both are only available these days as pattern items and they are usually correct for the model they were designed to fit, but mixtures of 1954 engines in, say, 1959 frames always create the headache of deciding whether to get a 1959 exhaust to suit the engine or a 1954 exhaust to suit the frame. Actually, either is a risk and probably neither will fit without modification.

As far as summing up my own enjoyment is concerned, I am a practical engineer and I take great pleasure in having vintage motorcycles that are in excellent mechanical condition and ready to ride anywhere and any time. Many

of my friends are people that I have met as a result of my Matchless motorcycles and my membership of the Owners Club. They come from many walks of life, which makes their acquaintance even more interesting. The machines themselves are comfortable to ride and their performance suits my riding style. What more could you ask?

BUYING

Any design produced for 28 years by an in volume motorcycle manufacturer ought to have something going for it and the Matchless G3 and G80 models described have an enviable record for reliability and finish. Equally, since they were early examples of badge engineering, there were many models, both AJS and Matchless singles and twins, which shared many common parts. In consequence there is a better than average supply of replacement parts available.

As with any vintage or classic motorcycle there are the inevitable pitfalls facing potential buyers, which were created by the popularity in ownership of such machines. Many unscrupulous owners performed very commendable looking restorations in order to achieve a better price but many of those restorations were made with incorrect mixtures of parts from various models and years. This will create many problems in years to come in trying to purchase replacement spares to either fit the hybrids or get them back to original specification.

Perhaps the worst examples of expensive but totally incorrect restorations are seen amongst the competition models. Many restorations for profit were made in a competition model format since,

by and large, they fetch better prices than roadsters of the same year, and also because the most difficult spares to find are the pressed sheet metal components like mudguards, toolboxes and chainguards. These components suffer naturally from rusting and were scrapped or replaced by incorrect units. Often they were damaged when over-zealous owners dropped their machines and many items were thrown away when the popular craze to convert all models to a cafe racer format was the vogue. It is not difficult to see that it is easier to fit alloy guards and an upswept exhaust together with one of the alloy petrol tanks which are still available rather than hunt out the correct roadster parts. Sadly, the competition models always differed significantly from the roadsters and a machine based upon a road engine – even if fitted with an alloy barrel – will be virtually unrideable on the rough. It is a bitter lesson to learn *after* you have parted with a small fortune.

There are even replica competition models being manufactured with the correct frame dimensions, the right looking petrol tank – frequently manufactured in fibreglass which prevents the legal use of the machine on the road – and the whole machine looking very much the part. Regrettably, they only look the part, since they do not have the correct trials wide ratio gear clusters, and the magnetos frequently fitted are the standard road units rather than the correct waterproofed Lucas 'Wader' instrument. The net result is that the gearing prevents their use in competition, as does the water-prone magneto. The fibreglass petrol tank makes their use on the road questionable.

With the purchase of any model, be it in concours condition or as a pile of rusting parts, 'caveat emptor' is the golden rule and you either have to really know your Matchless singles, really know the person from whom you are buying

the machine or thoroughly research the models beforehand. It is always advisable to seek an expert second opinion.

Once you have selected your machine there are very few replacement items that are completely unobtainable. Members of the AJS and Matchless Owners Club are likely to benefit most when seeking spares because the monthly journal, the 'Jampot', usually contains a series of useful advertisements from fellow members often offering spares for exchange. That isn't to say that all spares are readily available for many can be obtained that will keep the model running quite satisfactorily whilst you seek the precise replacement. Typical are the fibreglass mudguards which are virtually undetectable in use and often preferred by hard-riding owners who use their machines all year round.

One basic problem area for the uninitiated is that concerning the flywheel assembly. The factory made a two-piece crank-pin, with the pin made from a steel of excellent strength and a sleeve, with less strength but excellent wear properties. Most pattern replacements are manufactured as one-piece assemblies, which means that the machined junction of the step on the pin has to be radiused to retain the strength of the pin. The original assembly, with the sleeve, was not radiused so that it is essential to machine the flywheels to clear the radius. When the reconditioning work is undertaken by the crankpin manufacturer, as in the case of Alpha Bearings, this is standard practice, but if the work is committed to a general engineer who might not be aware of the small design difference, the likelihood of a subsequent early crankpin failure is high.

Apart from ensuring that all parts fitted are of the correct year of manufacture – there are subtle differences in the oilway layouts in some cases – there is little in the

Matchless longstroke single to give rise for concern. Care should be taken in the replacement of the oil pump and guide pin since cross-threading the latter is very likely to result in premature wear of the pump coupled with smashing the worm on the timing side axle in the extreme case. The whole pump area needs very careful reassembly and scrupulous attention to cleanliness since the pump works directly in the crankcase, steel bearing on to alloy. Dirt on the pump which damages the alloy crankcase is not unknown. At the time of writing it is worth inspecting the oil pump and guide pin very closely on 1947 models, since these components differ from those fitted before and after, and they are not available at the moment.

The pre-alternator models used a pressed steel primary chaincase with a rubber band and alloy covering strip. In the days before the Trades Description Act, the factory described the rubber band as a sealing strip, which it most certainly isn't! The chaincases frequently leak and the cures are legion. One popular cure is to use self-vulcanising rubber bead on one edge, others involve the use of many additional sealing compounds, often poured in whilst molten and allowed to set in place. One such cure recommends placing the machine on a see-saw then pouring molten tallow into the case and simultaneously rocking the see-saw to distribute the tallow ...

One point often overlooked is that the alloy chaincase models used open outer crankshaft bearings which allowed the engine to breathe freely into the chaincase.

Many owners mistakenly fit a main bearing with a single shield on the outside. To summarise, there are no serious problems to avoid and almost all models are readily available. If you are contemplating purchase of a concours model at inflated prices then you are strongly recommended to seek a second opinion. Some of the spectacularly attractive examples that have been presented in concours exhibitions and displayed from time to time in some of the specialist journals bear particular witness to careless research by the restorer. All too frequently it is forgotten that some of the Press Releases of years gone by were based on photographs of models which were intended for production yet never saw the light of day in the depicted format. Thus restorations are sometimes made which result in a perfect copy of the detail seen only in the Press Release.

CLUBS, SPECIALISTS & BOOKS

Clubs

The AJS and Matchless Owners Club has a membership of around sixteen hundred at the time of writing. Almost twenty per cent live outside the United Kingdom and there are active branches in Germany, the United States and Australia. There is also a completely separate club using the same motif based in Holland. Within the United Kingdon there are twenty three sections, each meeting at least once a month and often twice a month. All members receive a monthly journal which is a professionally printed, quality publication, with a wealth of photographs. The journal includes not only details of the Club's social events but also articles of technical, general and humorous content. There are specific technical tips and items of advice and assistance in the correspondence columns.

The major social function is the 'Jampot Rally' where members and their families meet in a camping weekend at a different location each year. It is not unusual to attract upwards of a thousand enthusiasts. A feature is always a run through the local countryside with mandatory inclusion of any models which are entered for the club's Concours d'Elegance. 'Ride Them Don't Hide Them', is the call.

There have been two hundred machines on the run.

There are also 'Jampot Rally' events in the United States and Autralia as well as an annual 'International' rally in Europe.

The Club has a Spares Scheme whereby items that are no longer available from commercial sources are manufactured and sold to members only. From time to time stocks of both new and second-hand spares have also been purchased by the Spares Scheme so the range of spares is high. Additionally, there is co-operation between the club and the trade suppliers and lists of spares are published from time to time in the club journal with details of precisely which supplier has stocks of which item.

The Club has had totally accurate transfers made for all the post-war models and many of the earlier ones, whilst pattern transfers are available from other sources but rarely are they as accurate in detail.

Like all clubs, the Membership Secretary may change from time to time. At the time of publication the contact address is:

Mr. T. Corley, Trojan Finance, 13B Rowan Road, London SW16 5JF. An alternative address is:

The AJS and Matchless Owners Club, Spares Scheme, Trent Business Centre, Canal Street, Long Eaton, Nottingham NG10 4HQ.

Specialists

Commercially available spares can be obtained from:
Hamrax Motors, 328, Ladbroke Grove, London W10
Russell Motors, 125-127, Falcon Road, London SW11
Joe Francis Motors Ltd., 340, Footscray Road, New Eltham, London SE9
Pattern parts are available from:
Malcolm Lee, Andrew Engineering (Leigh) Ltd, Mather House, Mather Lane, Leigh, Lancs. WN7 2PW – manufacturers of engine bolt sets, wheel spindles, chainguards, etc.
Armours Ltd, 784, Wimborne Road, Moordown, Bournemouth – suppliers of exhaust systems, seats, gasket sets and general spares, levers, cables, etc.
Brian Hitchisson, Lyta, Vauxhall Place, Dartford, Kent – manufacturer of alloy tanks.
Adrian Moss, Belvedere Works, Chalford, Stroud, Glos. – supplier of competition parts.
Andy Molnar, Scotts Hill Cottage, Ware, Herts – specialist stainless steel parts.

Books

Useful books are:
Matchless, by Peter Hartley. Published in 1981 by Osprey Publishing Ltd, 12-14 Long Acre, London WC2E 9LB.
AJS and Matchless, The Post-war Models, by Roy Bacon. Published in 1983 by Osprey. (see above for address)
British Motorcycles Since 1950, Vol 1, by Steve Wilson. Published in 1982 by Patrick Stephens Ltd, Barr Hill, Cambridge.
Matchless Single Cylinder, by F.W. Neill. Five editions published by C. Arthur Pearson between 1948 and 1960.
Now out of print. This is the 'bible', written by the factory Service Manager.
Xerox copies of Service Manuals/Riders Handbooks are

available from **Bruce Main-Smith Retail Ltd,** P.O. Box 20, Leatherhead, Surrey.
Matchless 1957-1964 Workshop Instruction Manual. The official factory publication available in Xerox copy reprints from Russell Motors, address as above (see Specialists).
Matchless 1939 – 1955, 350 and 500 cc Heavyweight Singles. A Bruce Main-Smith reprint of the

Motor Cycling Maintenance Series first published by Temple Press in 1958. Address as above.
Guide to Postwar British Motor Cycles, by C.J. Ayton. Published by The Hamlyn Publishing Group, 1982.
The Restoration of Vintage and

Thoroughbred Motorcycles, by Jeff Clew. Published in 1976 by Haynes Publishing Group, Sparkford, Yeovil, Somerset, BA22 7JJ

PHOTO GALLERY

1. The last of an era. The 40G3/WO used the current civilian Matchless frame with the 1940 Model 16 AJS engine.

1

2. Details of the 40G3/W0's girder fork. Note the 7 inch diameter brake and the bottom mudguard stay which doubles as a front stand.

2

3

4

5

6

3. Before War Office criticisms of weight. The Model 16-derived engine uses a heavily finned cylinder head and barrel. The exhaust pipe clamps to a stub.

4. A nearside view of the 40G3/W0 shows the larger diameter brake drum housing the speedometer drive.

5. The 40G3/W0 was not supplied with passenger equipment or panniers as standard. When these were required, a special rack was fitted to provide the room The tag on the cylinder base flange indicates the bore is oversize.

needed. The stop lamp switch on this machine has been fitted to comply with modern MOT requirements.

6. For some unknown reason, two toolboxes were fitted to the 40G3/W0 model as standard, whereas the civilian models made do with one. The extra rear lamp has been fitted to permit regular road use.

7

7. A standard WD identification plate shows this 40G3/W0 model did not require a base overhaul until 1955.

8. The 'big wing' Matchless motif on the 40G3/W0 petrol tank. The machine's civilian origins are further demonstrated by the integral sidecar lug on the front downtube, discarded on the later G3/L model.

8

9. Rider's eye view. An interesting feature of the 40G3/WO model is the cup holding the speedometer, cast into the top link assembly of the front fork. Rubber perishes in the presence of anti-personnel gases, so canvas grips were fitted.

10. The first of a line. The Don R's favourite mount was the W41G3/L with its lightweight telescopic front fork and good ground clearance. All machines of this type are known as 41G3/Ls, no matter in which year they were built.

9

10

11. One toolbox sufficed for the W41G3/L and the use of a smaller (3 pint) oil tank from the 250 helped save a little more weight. The exhaust pipe is of smaller diameter and is tucked out of harm's way behind the footrest.

12. By contrast with the 40G3/WO model, the W413G3/L specification included panniers and pillion fittings. The 'Camden' pillion pad is an early fitting, which was soon replaced by simpler versions.

13

13. The small diameter front brake, borrowed from the G2 250, is almost hidden by the fork slider. The petrol tank carries neither badges not knee grips, yet again to save weight. The cable sheath is a non-standard but novel modification.

14. The patent 'Teledraulic' front fork and the miniscule front brake fitted to the W41G3/L model. Comparison with photograph 1 will show the frame assembly is new and not, as is frequently suggested, that of the 40G3/W0 model fitted with telescopic forks.

15. The 41G3/L engine, where every effort has been made to reduce weight, employed a push-fit exhaust pipe (to save the weight of a clamp?).

14

15

16. The rider's eye view of the 41G3/L model shows the altogether much tidier aspect of the handlebar lug. Its puny two-stud clamp was not continued long after the war.

16

17. A 1955 G80S in close-to-original condition.

17

18. The famous 'Jampot' rear suspension unit. AMC's own product, it was basically a condensed Teledraulic fork leg. The full-width alloy hub is a quickly detachable design, introduced in 1955.

19. The opposite view. The 1955 rear brake plate is painted, but later versions were enclosed by a chrome-plated cover. The flare on the chainguard is a hang-over from the non-QD days, but the rear footrest bracket is new.

20. The Burman B52 gearbox, used from 1952 to 1956, with its unusual rotary gear indicator and no external clutch push-rod adjustment. Photograph 15 shows the earlier CP gearbox, and the 1958 G80S model features the AMC-Norton unit.

18

19

20

21. This engine has an alloy cylinder head and a
forward-mounted Lucas SR1 rotating magnet magneto.
Some restorers have not realised that the auto-advance
units for the 350 and 500 engines use different springs,
since they appear identical to the casual observer.

22

23

22. The full-width alloy hub looks better than its single-sided predecessors, but has only the same sized brake. On later models, the operating arm is diametrically opposite.

23. That much-cursed pressed steel chaincase! The clutch cover is removable for push rod adjustment and maintenance on this version. Only with the advent of RTV sealants can the leakage problem be overcome.

24. The smooth lines of the 1955 G80S can be seen here. The headlamp shell and the external pilot lamps were a Matchless feature for several years, but the hexagonal fork tube bolts with their domed covers are found only on 1955 models.

24

25

26

27

25. Points for the restorer. This machine has the correct dimensions for the tank lining and the correct plastic motif with the narrow outer ring, features frequently seen in error. The common, broad-edged plastic motif was used only in 1961. The narrow silver and red pinstripes were introduced in 1952. Note the handy steering lock!

26. The leakproof alloy chaincase, introduced with the alternator in 1958.

27. The 1957-on toolbox lids and oil tanks returned to the small laurel leaf transfer and have gold lines on the ribs for emphasis.

28

29

30

28. The non-standard Girling suspension unit fitted by AMC has an alloy clevis bottom fixing. It was fitted on all road and scrambles models from 1957 to 1962.

29. Almost the end of the line. The only major change subsequent to the 1958 G80S was the adoption of the duplex frame. The only non-AMC part on this machine is the rear carrier.

30. The last of the many. The 1963 layout has separate lighting and ignition switches. Practical features include the cable guides in the handlebar lug and rubber inserts in the fork bolts to reduce the ingress of water.

31

32

33

31. The 1963 'intermediate' front wheel has a new hub and an 18 inch diameter rim. The brake is much wider and the backplate has a water-excluding lip. Ball bearings were fitted in place of the taper rollers used for 30 years.

32. The new UK registration marks for 1963 required a wider rear number plate to accommodate the four digits. The unusual silencer was introduced in the same year and manages to be quieter, yet less obstructive.

33. Amongst numerous minor changes for 1963 were a new shape for the toolbox and oil tank, a swinging arm taking standard Girling units and a rear chainguard with a fully-enclosed option. Note how the stop lamp switch has been moved to the rear of the brake pedal.

34. A bike for the enthusiasts, not the purists. Jim Forrester's home-brewed special, based on a competition engine in a lightened road frame, seen crossing a river in the 1983 Scarborough Two-Day British Bike Trial.

34

35

36

37

35. The definitive enthusiast, Gerry Holdstock, riding his Matchless 350 in the 1983 Arbuthnot Trophy Trial. Gerry bought the bike in 1953 when it was just a year old, and has ridden it in active competition ever since.

36. A nice restoration of an early fifties trials model.

37. Mike Vangucci, of the Vintage Motor Cycle Club, eases his 1946 Model G80 to the top of a section in the Talmag Trophy Trial.

38. Action from one of the better-known pre-65 trials, the Talmag Trophy Trial, held in the Aldershot area on the third Sunday of January each year. Roger Sutton with his 1950 G3C in the 1984 event.

39. A regular competitor in vintage and classic trials, Mick Bull, with his own copy of an early fifties trials model.

40. A scrambles special with a sense of humour! All Matchless models with the forward magneto have kidney-shaped timing covers, and all AJS have an oval cover – except this one.

41

41. Planning a suitable sand-racing track as an added
attraction to the Isle of Man TT Races, Barry Briggs
borrowed a Matchless-based special to test the surface.

42. These Plumstead 'sisters', each well over 25 years` old, were used to tour through Germany and on to the Austrian Tyrol.

42

43. Les Stacey's machine seen at the Jampot Rally in Hertfordshire in 1981, when it won the Concours d'Elegance as the best single.

43

44. Early Sunday morning at the 1982 Jampot Rally in Lincolnshire as some of the 200 members of the Owners Club who took part in a road run prepare to set out. Open to members only, the annual rally is a 'must' for the Matchless enthusiast.

44

45. Not all members of the Owners Club are purist restorers, as this personalised model with extra stainless steel and chrome shows. The Club is renowned for its friendly atmosphere.

45

46. A rare find. The mud-spattered engine of a
Matchless home-brewed trials special. Of particular
interest is the Alfin alloy cylinder barrel, one of the units
sold to convert iron engines. The recognition point is the
exposed flange stud and nut.

C1

C1. In wartime matt finish, this W41G3/L could be waiting for her despatch rider. The silencer is not standard and is welded to the exhaust pipe.

C2. A W41G3/L rolling chassis.

C2

C3. The Type 275 Amal carburettor cannot be removed until the bell mouth has been taken off. The Lucas dynamo, lurking behind the magneto chaincase, was the bane of mechanics.

C4. By the mid-fifties, AMC had smoothed out the lines of the machine by blending tanks, seat and toolbox. Red beading on the seat shows it is for a Matchless.

C3

C4

C5. The loss of the magneto chaincase leaves a lot of space around the cylinder, to the regret of many enthusiasts. The folding kickstarter crank is in error; touring models were supplied with the fixed version.

C6. Balanced by the horn and magneto, the engine sits solidly in the frame of this 1955 model. The tank motif is incorrect but is widely used. Members of the Owners Club can now obtain the real thing for the first time in many years.

C7. An aspect familiar to many motorcyclists – a 'Jampot' and a small toolbox. Note the small bolt at the base of the twinseat.

C5

C6

C7

C8. For 1956 attempts were made to style the roadsters with a longer but shallower seat, and a long, slim toolbox with corresponding oil tank. It is no wonder this transfer was used for one year only!

C9. Like many other manufacturers, AMC used painted wheel rims for many years. The options were black or red, lined with silver. The 1955 fork slider is still angular but has lost the front mudguard stay mount.

C10. Is there any doubt that they were Matchless?

C8

C9

C10

C11

C11. 35 very good reasons for joining the AJS and Matchless Owners Club! The spares scheme can offer members full sets of transfers back to the 1930s.

C12. All dressed up and somewhere to go! These singles should be giving pleasure to their owners for years to come, on the road where they belong.

C12

C13. With the exception of the 1951 competition models, three types of gearbox were used on the G3 and G80 singles:
(left to right) Burman CP to 1951, Burman B52 to 1956 and the in-house AMC gearbox from 1957.

C14. The CP gearbox is a sound, if ponderous, design. Ex-WD versions are marked 8CPBL (CP Bottom Low) and do not have rollers in the gear selector camshaft.

C15. B52 gearboxes have a lighter change than the CPs, as there are fewer dogs to engage. Note the drum-shaped selector cam at the bottom right and the clutch operating mechanism in the outer case (AJS and Matchless Owners Club)

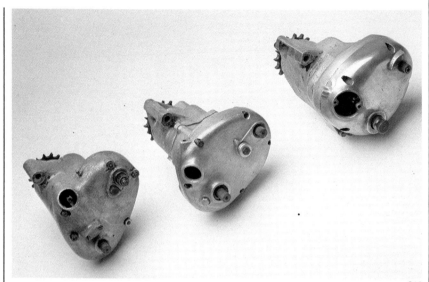

C13

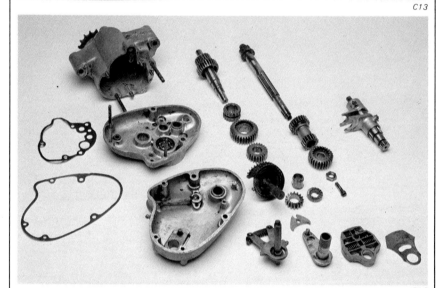

C14

C15

C16

C17

C18

C16. The AMC gearbox is renowned for its ability to transmit a great deal of power, but early models were plagued by selector spring fractures. 1962-on versions have a different kickstarter return spring.

C17. The same basic design was used on both AMC (AJS and Matchless) and Norton models from late 1956. AMC gearboxes are identified by an 'M' prefix to the number and Norton by an 'N'. Since the mounting points differ, the cases do not interchange.

C18. Plating restrictions were still in force for UK models in 1953, so the front brake plate is Argenised. (Keith Jackson)

C19. The alloy cylinder barrel has had fins removed for a rear-mounted magneto. The chrome-plated chaincase is pretty, but non-standard, as is the carburettor. (Keith Jackson)

C20. All frames built up to 1955 could have either rigid or sprung rear ends. The swinging arm pivot is housed in the large alloy casting to the front of the rear mudguard; it is usually painted. (Keith Jackson)

C19

C20